Passive Income

Escape the 9 to 5, build passive income and live location free.

Beginners Guide to Creating Multiple Streams of Income without Having to

Work in Them.

Table of Contents

Introduction

Earn money while sleeping. That is the ultimate dream right? And while to most people, this sounds like nothing but a good dream; to the lucky ones, that is a way of living. Wait before you put down your kindles or scroll to a new page. This is not one of those shady, scammy books that will promise you a fortune and feed off your "not-so-satisfactory financial situation." This is a book that will ultimately change your life. No upfront fees required, no fancy courses needed to be purchased. This book will put more money in your bank account, give you more freedom to live anywhere you want and join the rich.

If you are looking for a way to become a millionaire overnight, let me break it to you, there isn't one. If you came here simply looking for a quick get-rich scheme, this isn't the book for you. But if you are willing to get your hands a little bit dirty so you can lay back and collect the dollars later, then this guide will get you there. Serving the best passive income streams with the lowest risk, this guide will show you how doing a little bit of work upfront can easily get you off your never-ending 9 to 5 grind, and help you live the life of your dreams – work little from anywhere and at any time.

Real Estate Investing

Do you know the saying "it takes money to make money"? Well, whoever thought of that was surely financially independent. Obviously, the most profitable way to increase your bank account is if you have some money one the side, waiting to be invested in something (but don't worry, if you are in a financial struggle and live paycheck to paycheck; the next chapters will show you how you can generate passive income with little or no money).

Buying a Property

Despite the unexpected ups and downs that are known to hit real estate occasionally, this investment is still by far the most lucrative way to receive serious returns in the long run. And you don't have to be a real estate tycoon to taste the benefits of this profitable investment. All it takes is to invest in a 20-percent down payment for a property. Have some money saved for the rainy days? Well, guess what? If you are reading this book, there is already a cloud over your head. Make simple calculations, and you will see how productive this investment can be. Collecting the rental checks will not only pay your mortgage and give you a property that you can sell in 30 years and earn a pure profit of hundreds of thousands of dollars, but it will also bring some extra cash flow every month. If that is not an option to consider, I don't know what is.

Let's assume that you are about to buy a $100,000 property. You make a down payment of $20,000 and take a 30-year loan with a fixed interest rate of 4 percent. You borrow $80,000 from the bank, and once you do the calculations, you will see that your mortgage will be $382. Your taxes and insurance will most likely be approximately $170 on average, so your total monthly expenses will be around $552. If you choose to rent out your property for $800 a month, your positive cash flow will be $248. Not to mention the fact that after 30 years you get to sell the property.

However, know that being a landlord has a way of bringing you headaches. From inconsiderate tenants, occasional vacant properties, to minor repairs, and dealing with rent increasements, not everyone is cut out to be a landlord. Just something to think about.

Crowdfunding

Buying a property is great, for those who have the money to make a down payment, that is. But what about the majority of people who are struggling to extend their monthly budget and cannot afford to set aside 20 percent of the property's price? Those of you who don't have the money to buy a property, but would love to reap the passive income that owning a real estate can bring, should think about real estate crowd funding.

Real estate crowdfunding is probably the safest passive income option there is. This is even better than buying and renting a property because in this case, you don't have to be a landlord, or deal with the inconveniences that owning a property can bring. All that this hands-off investment requires is for you to invest some money, sit back, and receive the returns.

This more affordable option has become a real hit lately since it allows you to become a property owner with as little as a $1,000 investment. The best site to consider is www.fundrise.com where you can earn more than 10% of annual dividends. Obviously, the more you invest, the more cash flow you get. That may not seem like a lot if you have only $1,000 to invest, but in the long run, you can earn a lot. Plus it beats the interest rates on your savings account right? So why keep your money in the bank when you can actually invest them?

Peer-to-Peer Landing

Yes, I know what you think. Another method that involves serious cash. But don't be so quickly dismissive and bear with me on this one. I promise you will thank me at the end.

When it comes to making safe investments, probably the most reliable and least risky method is to invest in your government. We are all familiar with the US Treasury securities, and there is no doubt that your money will be safe and sound, giving you a great piece of mind. But the one thing you need and this investment will not provide you with, are good returns. The safest investments such as this one will not provide you with more than 1% of returns, which is a passive income, but let's face it, is simply not worth the trouble.

But, drumroll... deciding to invest in a Lending Club, on the other hand, now that is something that can surely pay a couple of bills. Lending Club is an online platform for peer to peer lending where people in need come to take loans that people who are looking for an extra way to earn, provide. It may not sound like the most humane thing to do, earning from other people's problems, but the truth is, that's how this world works. I know people who used to struggle with this one until they finally realized that if they weren't providing that money, those in need would never be able to solve their financial problems. So, there's that.

But really, emotions on the side, the Lending Club can be a great source to maximize the income, without having to work for it.

If you have heard some bad words about these investments, it is probably because they carry a particular risk. Some investments could go bad, indeed, but not if you are smart enough to divide and organize your investments in a way that would not backfire financially. According to the Lending Club's advisers, the safest amount to invest is $2500. But there is a trick to it. You don't invest the whole deposit at once but buy into one hundred $25 loans. That way if an investment was doomed to go bad, losing $25 would not hurt you financially.

The interests rates that the Lending Club offer vary, but they are always substantial. Obviously, the more you invest, the more you will earn, but whatever the deposit, you should be able to earn approximately 10 percent.

Affiliate Marketing

If you have spent some time online searching for ways to earn passive income, then chances are, you have already come across the term affiliate marketing. And while this is a term that is practically on the verge of becoming just another buzzword, the truth is, not that many people know the meaning of it.

Affiliate marketing, if you ask me, is one of the greatest ways to create passive income. Why? Because you don't actually have to build or make anything. What you do, is sell others products. There was a time when things were simpler, receiving commission from door-to-door sales, today that is done way more passively. A great platform is all you need to start building your passive income wealth.

If you own a blog or consider starting one, affiliate marketing is the best way to turn your blog into a money-making machine. If you are not into blogging, do not worry, that does not mean that you cannot choose this passive income method. In that case, you will need to create a website where you can review and promote the products, and offer links where the potential buyers can buy them from. But don't let this stress you out, there are tons of free website providers you can create your own website in no time, even without a prior experience.

Choosing the Network

But where do you find these products? Just like a small-store owner who has to choose his merchandise from a trustworthy seller for a fair price, an affiliate marketer has to find the best network to choose his products from. There are many networks available that offer different services, so be careful and make sure that the one you choose to join in will bring you the most benefit.

Here are some of the best affiliate networks at this time:

Amazon Associates. Amazon is more than just the place you find great deals and buy discounted things. Amazon is the largest retailer in the world and can also help you draw more traffic to your site and blog by providing you with affiliate links.

This affiliate network gives you access to the millions of great products sold on Amazon, for free. That's right you can join Amazon Associates for free where you can choose the products you want to advertise to your potential buyers.

To answer the question that I'm pretty sure you're asking yourself at this moment, Amazon gives you 4 to 9 percent of commission per product, of course, depending on the size of the affiliate.

The only thing that perhaps draws affiliate marketers away from this network is Amazon's strict policy to pay marketers 60 days after the sale has been made.

Check out their website and get started https://affiliate-program.amazon.com/welcome/getstarted.

Rakuten Affiliate. If you are looking for a network that has been in the business the longest, then this is the one. Not only has Rakuten been successfully working since 1997, but this network also offers more than 1000 advertisers that you can partner with.

10

The network is super user-friendly and free to join, but the best part are the very attractive commissions. Unlike Amazon that pays up to 9 percent, Rakuten gives its affiliate marketers commissions that range between 8-15 percent. But that is not all. For every sold item Rakuten will also reward you with an additional $0.99. So why would anyone choose another network? The only drawback is that Rakuten's payment methods are somewhat unpredictable and can happen within a week or after 60 days. Plus, Rakuten does not offer a PayPal option.

If this sounds like a great deal to you, go to https://rakutenmarketing.com/affiliate.html for more info.

Click Bank. Another great affiliate network with 19 years of successfully providing its services, is Click Bank. Click Bank has been supplying affiliate marketers with full-time income for many years now, because of its high commission rates that can range from 1% to incredible 75%, as well as thanks to its 12,000 vendors.

Other great advantages are the fact that Click Bank is also free to join, and that it offers full technical and commercial customer support.

The disadvantage is that Click Bank has a more specific payment method policy. If 75 percent of commission sounds like the great reason to chose this network, you have to know that Click Bank will not pay you unless you have made at least 5 sales. To be even more restrictive, these sales have to be done from at least 2 payment methods (for instance one via PayPal and another via Master Card).

Check out their website for additional info http://www.clickbank.com/affiliate-network/.

Some other great affiliate networks that you should consider are:

- **Share a Sale** - http://shareasale.com/

- **Avant Link** - http://avantlink.com/

- **Affi Bank** - http://affibank.com/

Sponsored Content

The huge misconception is that affiliate marketing and selling sponsored content are the same. Although we must agree that they are somewhat similar, these two passive income methods represent two very different things.

After Facebook updated its Branded Content policy and officially approved verified news pages to post and sell sponsored content, it seems that this passive income strategy has rapidly begun to grow. But what exactly is sponsored content selling and how it is actually different than affiliate marketing?

Sponsored content is any content that you get paid to advertise. Wait, isn't that what affiliate marketing is? Actually no. Affiliate marketers place links of products on their sites without any guarantee that they will bring them money. They only get paid after someone purchases that product. Sponsored content, on the other hand, fills your pockets regardless of how many purchases you make. You get paid to advertise the content upfront, even if no one chooses to read it.

Great, where do I sign? If it were that easy everyone would do it. For a company or seller to pay you to advertise their content, you must already have a high platform with enough traffic. That means that you cannot simply create a website in no time and start receiving money to advertise content no one would ever see. You need a well-known blog or a website to get the opportunity to sell sponsored content.

By choosing to promote a content, you are advertising something that is paid to you by a brand, whether we are talking about a service or a physical product. How much can you earn by producing such content? Well, the sky is the limit. How much you are going to earn depends on many factors. It depends on how popular is your platform and most importantly, how valuable you are. If you already have a big audience that reads your posts and wants your advice, that makes you super valuable and gives you an extraordinary negotiating power that you have to consider using. My advice for you is to always start with a high figure and meet the brand somewhere in the middle. That's a far better option than to undervalue yourself, don't you think?

Here are some common tools and networks that you can communicate and negotiate with brands, and find some great sponsored content opportunities:

HubSpot (https://www.hubspot.com/partners) – If you use the HubSpot software for your blog, then this is the perfect network for you to find brands to pay you to promote their services.

Adproval (https://new.adproval.com/) – This is probably the best network where you can get connected with a brand and find a great deal.

IZEA (https://izea.com/) – If you are a social media influencer and have many followers, this marketplace will offer you some amazing ways to cash in your influence and earn extra money.

Blogvertise (https://www.blogsvertise.com/) – Another great marketplace for bloggers who want to get connected with brands and earn passive income by selling sponsored content.

BuySellAdds (https://www.buysellads.com/) – A great network where you can communicate with brands and find some amazing products and services that you can promote and earn money.

Online Courses

Is there anything you are particularly good at doing? There must be. Everyone has something that they can teach others. Think about it for a second. Whether it is something as impressive as impeccably drawing portraits or as simple as speaking your native language, there must be something that you know that some other people don't. Why not take advantage of that and use it as a great passive income source?

Who says you have to be a licensed teacher in order to teach people? You don't have to be born and bred Italian to teach others the language, either. All that is required of you is that you possess the knowledge that others are willing to pay to have. How? By making an online course.

The beauty of these online courses is not only in the fact that you don't need a license or previous teaching experience in order to teach but also in your full pockets. Is it possible for real teachers to be so underpaid, and for those selling online courses to make it up to $1,000 per hour? Yes, it says $1,000, not $10.00. As imaginable as it seems now, you can actually kiss your day job goodbye with this astonishing method. And the best part is that you do it passively. You don't actually have to teach the same lesson over and over again to students. No, you simply create the course upfront and place it online for sale so that students can enroll in and learn things that they do not know. That means that for 20-30 hours of work, you can actually earn tens of thousands of dollar in passive income. And it costs you the same. No matter if there are only 10 or 1000 students that are willing to buy your course, it will cost you the same. I hardly believe you could fit 1000 students in a single classroom to teach Italian. With these online courses, that is unlimited.

Where to Teach?

But where to teach? Can you put your online course on your website and make money out of it? Well, yes, if someone chooses to buy it. But why would someone choose you over those who choose to sell their courses from well-known teaching sites? That is the same as if you decided to teach from home instead of doing it in a popular school.

There are many platforms that people use to host their online courses on. Which one of those is best for you depends on your preferences, how skilled you are at designing, as well as the type, of course, you plan on selling. Go through this list carefully before committing yourself to a certain platform:

Udemy (https://teach.udemy.com) – Udemy definitely wears the crown for being the greatest online course platform you will find today. On this platform, there are over 20,000 instructors teaching courses to over 12 million students.
It is completely free to register and to create your online course on Udemy. The best part is that it is user-friendly so you don't need an expert level in technology to make a decent course.

So, where's the catch? The thing is that for every sold course, Udemy takes 50% of your earnings.

But, don't be too disappointed, the average teacher on Udemy earns approximately $7,000.

Skillshare (https://www.skillshare.com/) – This is another great platform that offers personalized help when it comes to customizing your courses. Unlike Udemy, Skillshares does not pay a fixed price, but the earnings depend on the minutes watched. The more minutes of the course the students watch, the more money you earn. Teachers on Skillshare make up to $40,000 a year.

Teachable (https://teachable.com/) – Although teachable isn't free to join, in my opinion, it is a better option than Udemy. Why? Primarily because of the earnings. The cheapest subscription plan on Teachable costs $39, and it takes only 5% off your earnings. If you ask me, that is a far better option for someone who is serious about selling online courses, than sharing 50% of all the earnings. And if you don't feel like sharing at all, you don't have to. With a $99 monthly subscription, Teachable won't taka a cent from your earnings. Isn't that something?

There are over 3 million active students on Teachable.

Other great platforms where you can sell your online courses are:

- **Ruzuku** - https://www.ruzuku.com/

- **Academy of Mine** - https://www.academyofmine.com/

- **WizIQ** - https://www.wiziq.com/

- **Learn Worlds** - https://www.learnworlds.com/

- **Thinkific** - https://www.thinkific.com/

Passive Income from Royalties

One of the greatest ways to generate passive income is to receive royalties on a regular basis, and literally, earn money while you sleep. Just imagine waking up in the morning just to realize that your bank account has grown. Wouldn't that be something?

For you to receive royalties, you have to have something to sell. But unlike selling physical products in a store where you have to refill the shelves once you sell some items, earning royalties online is an entirely different process. You earn royalties for the same product or digital content, regardless of the number of sales you make.

Selling eBooks

People quit their jobs and choose to do this instead. Selling eBooks can be quite the lucrative passive income stream, but only if you do it right. People have seriously retired by 40 with this method, so I strongly suggest you give it a shot.

First of all, writing a book, and writing a book that will sell are two very different things. Why? Because you are not writing about the topics that you like, but about something that readers would want to read. After all, they are the ones that bring you royalties. And while this may seem like too much of a hassle, believe me, with the right approach, it can be done within a day.

Here is what you have to know about creating passive income with eBooks:

Where to Start?

Like I said, the most important thing is to choose a topic that interests readers. Will it be fiction or nonfiction? Do some research and see what other authors are offering. Do not be intimidated by the competition, and be smart. If there isn't a similar topic on the market, that does not mean that writing a book of that kind will sell well; it usually means that people are not interested in that topic. You will have more chances of succeeding if you choose a niche that is crowded with authors (such as weight-loss), than something that people don't feel like reading.

Should You Write It Yourself?

If you are creative and have excellent writing skills, the only thing that you have to invest in order to create passive income this way is a portion of your time. If however, you know nothing about creating and giving the content a flow, it is best to hire someone else to do it for you. Many freelance writers can provide you with a good quality book without emptying your pocket. The best platform to find good writers is www.upwork.com.

What about the Cover?

The cover photo of the eBook is probably more important than the book itself since that is what hooks the readers and attracts them to click on the book's thumbnail. If the book does not start to sell well, changing the book cover is perhaps the smartest thing to do. If you cannot design a cover yourself, you can find some great designers on Upwork.

Where to Sell It?

The best platform to sell your eBook is definitely Amazon. We cannot argue the fact that Amazon currently is the dominator among the online retails, and choosing the Amazon Kindle Direct Publishing to publish your eBooks is the best option since is the only way to reach a large audience.

It costs absolutely nothing to publish a book on this platform, and you can earn 35% royalties from the sales if your book is priced below $2.99 or above $9.99, and incredible 75% if you choose to price it between $2.99 and $9.99. For more info visit their official site https://kdp.amazon.com/.

Although it is the best platform, there are also other sites besides Amazon where you can sell your eBooks:

- **PayHip** - https://payhip.com/

- **Lulu** - http://www.lulu.com/us/en/create/ebooks?cid=us_pubpage_ebooks/

- **SmashWords** - https://www.smashwords.com/about/how_to_publish_on_smashwords

- **Kobo** - https://www.kobo.com/writinglife

Do You Need Promotion?

Absolutely. Promoting the book is even more important than writing it. If you want to reach an audience, you better consider saving some money aside about book campaigns and promotion. Amazon offers you the chance to promote your book that way that you set a budget for your campaign, and anytime a potential reader clicks on your book, Amazon will deduct a fixed price from your budget.

If you don't know what you are doing and don't want to waste your time or money, you can also hire a freelancer to be your Kindle assistant and help you with book promotion.

Selling Stock Photos

Although every one of us secretly wishes to own a fancy camera to capture the most amazing moments ever, not everyone can afford to do so. But that shouldn't discourage you. If you take a look at your smartphone I am sure you will find some great photos that someone would want to purchase, whether we are talking about that yummy burger you had the other day or those flowers you took a picture of while walking in the park.

If you didn't already get the point, you don't have to be a professional to earn some extra cash passively. Pick some photos from your phone or set aside a few hours for taking a few pictures, and put them up online for sale.

There are many different platforms where you can sell your photos and earn royalties from:

Alamy (www.alamy.com). If you are looking for a great deal, then Alamy will surely give you one. Offering 50% of royalties to its photographs, this platform is a great way for you to increase your bank balance. But wait, it gets better. Alamy will not trick you into becoming exclusive, and you will be free to sell your photos on other platforms as well. Although the competition is high since Alamy offers 90 million photos, videos, and illustrations, with this platform's great demand almost everyone has a chance of earning some extra bucks.

Shutterstock (www.shutterstock.com). Shutterstock is, without a doubt, one of the greatest platforms for buying and selling stock photos. But, unlike Alamy, its payment policy is a little bit more complicated:

- For each photo that you sell as a single image, you will be paid 20% of the price.

- For each photo that you sell as a part of their 25-day subscription, you will be paid $0.25.

- For each photo that is bought by someone who has an on-demand-download subscription, you will get $1.88.

- For each photo that has been bought with an 'Enhance Download' subscription, you will receive $25.

Adobe Stock (www.adobestock.com). With over 4 million registered buyers and over 50 million photos, Adobe stock is another serious platform for selling stock photos. Their royalties of 22-46 % may not be the most attractive, but their no-threshold policy surely is. No threshold means that you will automatically get paid for each purchase and the site will not hold your money.

Selling Stock Music

To sell stock music, you don't have to be Elvis Presley and make the ultimate hits that will never die. The only thing you need to be able to increase the income you receive passively is to have some musical talent.

No, I am not talking about making a song either. You don't have to sell full songs for people to buy them. People buy short audio files all the time for all sorts of reason. The most lucrative way is if you choose to license the music you make.

Licensed music or stock music means that whenever someone buys your music you automatically give them the rights to use that file whether for private or commercial purposes (although that depends on the license you choose).

If you know how to sing or produce a decent music with an instrument, why not record it and put it up for sale? There is nothing for you to lose after all.

Here are some great platforms where you can sell your stock music:

Audio Jungle (www.audiojungle.com). When it comes to stock music, there is no other platform with such high demand. And while this is definitely worth considering, so is the fact that in order to sell music on Audio Jungle, your music must not be sold elsewhere. Audio Jungle offers 30% royalties.

Pond 5 (www.pond5.com). Although not as fancy as Audio Jungle, Pond 5 is another great place where you can sell your stock music, mostly because of their more acceptable payment policy. With Pond 5 you can earn 50% from every sale, plus you don't have to sell your music there exclusively.

Premium beat www.premiumbeat.com is another site that is worth considering.

Earn from YouTube

We have all heard stories or know someone who has been regularly making money from YouTube. But what not everybody knows is the fact that you don't actually have to be the next YouTube star in order to receive a substantial passive income from this leading video platform.

Want to try but don't know where to start? Follow these steps and start earning almost instantly:

Building Your Channel. Every account on YouTube has its own channel that is attached to it. Your YouTube account is the same as your Google account so you can either choose to use that existing one or create a new one.

- Make sure that you use Keywords that will help people discover your channel.

- Make sure to think of a short and original user name that people can easily remember.

- Describe yourself and your channel in a nutshell. This is an opportunity for you to tell people why they should subscribe and watch your videos so be creative.

Add Videos. Once you have a channel, it is time to add videos.

- Make sure that your videos are of high quality and aren't very long.

- Don't worry if they are not perfect. You will master this in time, and with each upload, you will be adding better and better content.

- Make sure to upload on a regular basis so you can keep your audience.

Gain Your Audience. The best way to gain audience is if you promote your videos on other platforms like Facebook or Twitter. Another great way is to communicate with your viewers in the comment section regularly.

Monetize the Content. Now, this is the part you have all been waiting for. For you to start receiving paychecks from YouTube, you will have to monetize your videos. That means that you allow YouTube to place ads in your video. To do so go to your channel, click on 'Video Manager' found on the top bar. Click on 'Channel' and then enable the monetization. You will start earning money only after your video gets 1,000 views.

Set Up the Google AdSense. Go to the Ad Sense website, sign up and create an account. To do so, you will need to use a valid email address and enter a bank account or PayPal information.

Now, know that this is pay per click, which means that you will get a really small amount after someone clicks on the ad in your video, but over time, these little amounts can really add up, especially if you have a wide audience and many views.

Checking the Analytics. After you monetize your site, set up Google AdSense, and start getting views, you can check how your videos are performing simply by clicking on the Analytics button in your Channel menu.

Become a YouTube Partner. When someone says they are earning well from YouTube they usually mean that they have a really large audience and many, many views. To start earning from this platform this way, you will have to become a partner. No, I don't mean that you will own a portion of YouTube. YouTube partners are those members who have a large number of viewers. These partners get pay per the number of views, as well as have access to many more creation tools and community support.

In order to become a YouTube partner you have to have at least 15,000 watch hours in the last 90 days.

Seem like something your videos can pull of? Why not upload your content today?

Conclusion

This isn't a book that will make you an overnight millionaire. This is a book that will help you step away from the 9 to 5 grind and enable you to use the power of internet and today's technology to earn money without having to report to no one else but yourself.

Does it sound like too good to be truth? Why not try these amazing passive income ideas today and let me convince you otherwise?

www.ingramcontent.com/pod-product-compliance
Lightning Source LLC
Chambersburg PA
CBHW061239180526
45170CB00003B/1365